# HAPPINESS IS...

# A WARM PUPPY

## BY
## CHARLES
## M.
## SCHULZ

First paperback edition 1971
Revised, expanded paperback edition 1983
Reprint of revised, expanded paperback edition 1990

Based on "Happiness is a Warm Puppy"
by Charles M. Schulz

Published by Determined Productions, Inc.
Box 2150, San Francisco, CA 94126
Printed in Hong Kong

ISBN 0-915696-75-4
Library of Congress Catalog Card No. 79-63489

The first edition of HAPPINESS IS A WARM PUPPY appeared in 1962. It was an immediate hit and topped the national best-seller lists for forty-five weeks. Well over a million copies were sold.

Now, world-famous cartoonist Charles M. Schulz, who wrote and illustrated the original little volume, is back with his new and enlarged edition of HAPPINESS IS A WARM PUPPY

The revised version, all in color, contains three times as many pages, full of new drawings and new sentiments.

Snoopy and the entire PEANUTS® gang are on hand again — all of which promises a whole lot of fun as well as a whole lot of HAPPINESS!

Be sure to ask for the new and enlarged edition of LOVE IS WALKING HAND-IN-HAND, also by Mr. Schulz.

# Happiness is knowing who you are.

# Happiness is watching an old movie.

# Happiness is getting together with your friends.

# Happiness is a new jogging suit.

# Happiness is finding someone you like at the front door.

# Happiness is
# lots of candles.

# Happiness is
a pile
of leaves.

# Happiness is
# a waterbed.

# Happiness is disco dancing.

# Happiness is taking three airline stewardesses to lunch.

# Happiness is
# a night light.

# Happiness is
one dollar
for the movie,
35 cents for popcorn
and 15 cents
for a candy bar.

# Happiness is finding out you're not so dumb after all.

# Happiness is finding the little piece with the pink edge and part of the sky and the top of the sail boat.

# Happiness is knowing how to tie your own shoes.

# Happiness is a piece of fudge caught on the first bounce.

# Happiness is a good old-fashioned game of hide and seek.

# Happiness is knowing all the answers.

# Happiness is
# show and lie.

# Happiness is a smooth sidewalk.

# Happiness is climbing a tree.

# Happiness is walking in the grass in your bare feet.

# Happiness is a camping trip.

# Happiness is sleeping in your own bed.

# Happiness is scarfing junk food.

**Happiness is
three friends
in a sandbox...
with no fighting.**

# Happiness is an umbrella and a new raincoat.

# Happiness is standing around waiting for the chicks.

# Happiness is having someone to solve your problems.

PSYCHIATRIC HELP 5¢

THE DOCTOR IS **IN**

# Happiness is the hiccups... after they've gone away.

# Happiness is a warm puppy.

# Happiness is a blow-dry hairdo.

# Happiness is remote control T.V.

# Happiness is knowing you have a pretty face.

# Happiness is a thumb and a blanket.

# Happiness is forty-nine flavors.

# Happiness is finding a caddy who doesn't fall into the hole.

# Happiness is flying south for the winter.

# Happiness is expecting someone special.

# Happiness is eating out.

# Happiness is sharing.

# Happiness is
# a cat nap.

# Happiness is
# a new
# bicycle.

# Happiness is an invitation to a party.

# Happiness is sunlight, air, plants, water, soil, birds, microorganisms...

# Happiness is finding someone to type your term paper.

# Happiness is reaching the top.

# Happiness is mellow.

# Happiness is overcoming your fears.

# Happiness is an "A" on your spelling test.

# Happiness is living in a high-rise.

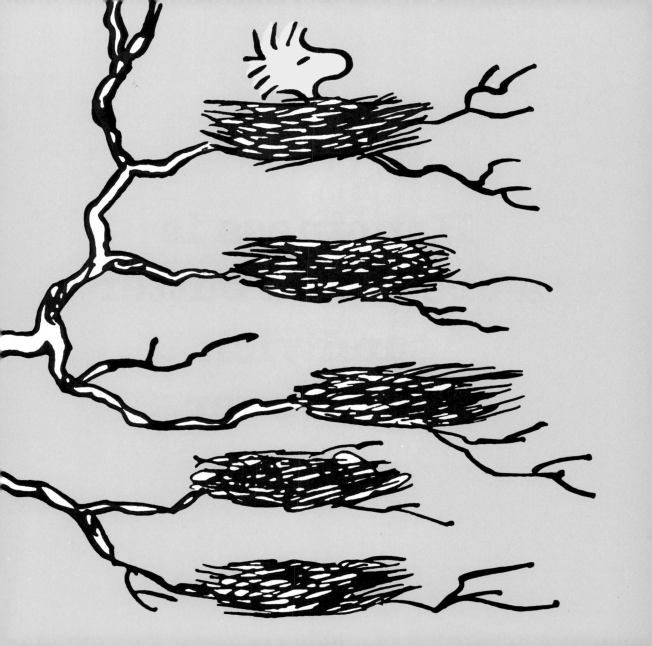

# Happiness is a bread and butter sandwich folded over.

# Happiness is eighteen different colors.

# Happiness is storing up solar energy.

# Happiness is winning a trophy.

# Happiness is being glad you're you.

# Happiness is getting to the semi-finals.

# Happiness is having an audience.

# Happiness is your first kiss in the rain.

# Happiness is finally getting the splinter out.

# Happiness is being able to reach the doorknob.

# Happiness is
one thing
to one person
and another thing
to another
person.